T0159095

The Queen's
Mansion Full Module

EVANGELINE CAIN

authorHOUSE®

AuthorHouse™
1663 Liberty Drive
Bloomington, IN 47403
www.authorhouse.com
Phone: 1 (800) 839-8640

Published by AuthorHouse   01/17/2019

ISBN: 978-1-5462-7596-1 (sc)
ISBN: 978-1-5462-7595-4 (e)

Print information available on the last page.

Any people depicted in stock imagery provided by Getty Images are models, and such images are being used for illustrative purposes only. Certain stock imagery © Getty Images.

This book is printed on acid-free paper.

Because of the dynamic nature of the Internet, any web addresses or links contained in this book may have changed since publication and may no longer be valid. The views expressed in this work are solely those of the author and do not necessarily reflect the views of the publisher, and the publisher hereby disclaims any responsibility for them.

Chapter One

Message from Venus

Hi, I am mother Venus the goddess of the land. My domain is love, peace, and light and if you are looking to rise above the ashes of ignorance or manifests new abundance into your life I am your guide. I my loves, have put in tireless efforts to pull you into my web of light that stems within my womb, because I know you've heard the call within, you've even felt something pulling on your heart strings and tried to distinguish what it is.

You know that from the well of our chalice your womb knows who you really are. She knows your ancient feminine power that lives on. She awakes my loves; she claims extended love and spreads it far and wide. She rises, walks in the close that resembles me with love encoded in her blood. She knows, she has a unique soul contract to fill and rises to the activation of her calling.

My dearest daughters and sons, I send you celestial blessings from afar. I am here today as representation of the goddess, because I have been told through the heavens that humanity is at a breaking point and people are finding it hard to bypass negative energies.

The forces of Venus are being opposed by negative energies that I will prevail and prove that I am more powerful than any opposing force:

She, the gatekeeper only stands for love, therefore all else is corrupt. She is the law of light and no darkness can find its way inside the temple of my heart. She is a timeless muse who is never forgotten, rooted in love that goes back in time and protects us.

1

We say:

Oh Venus, goddess of love, the woman to whom a thousand temples rise. The goddess gowned by silken wraps, her title known as lap of luxury..

Venus, when the cave of darkness tries to pull us in we shall build a starship to take us directly to you for you awaken heartfelt emotions. The woman who gifts us with spiritual nutrition. She, the womb who provides the land with milk & honey. i know that you are the guardians put on this sacred earth to create heaven on earth. You are the clay that molded to hold within you love, peace, humility, honour, and respect for all beings.

Venus the goddess of love has asked me to carry a message of truth to you today. Her first response was thank you, thank you for not denying me my sons and daughters. She asked that you bring back the divine feminine in you, the feminine who has been lost and searching trying to find her way home to self. She has asked, that you unveil your mask and follow her instructions into an unfamiliar path. A path that is fruitful with promise, a path that holds the love that is encoded in your heart and to rise up my dear one to conquer all illusions and fear..

You are asked to look within and open the gardens of your heart and follow the authority that is being given to you, because the world awaits to plant your seeds of intention and so I ask you to defend your ancestors and carry their codes of love to dry earth.

I ask, that you never deny me and to always defend my name for I am the mother of the earth who's protected you for thousands of years. I have left an image of me in you, so you can walk in my image. As you come to recognize me you will come to know inner peace and rest. As you walk dressed as me you will discover that you are in the mist of experiencing a great transition into the fertile soil that incubates what is next to grow.

Inanna

Chapter Two

Inanna is rising my loves. She rises cloaked in the silk garnets of all of life's creation. She says," bow down to me for I am the gatekeeper of mysteries and wisdom untold...

Do you hear me speak to you dear ones?

Should you dare to look inside the secrets of the doors where I reside, than, and only then will you see me waiting for you.

Do you feel my presence there dear one?

My sister Sophia, the avatar the cosmic queen has arrived to hover over you and shelter you like a blanket, to carry you away from the ego and teach you spiritual alignment.

Come my dears, I have been waiting for you. Waiting for you to feel the warm that lives inside of me that has been sheltered from you.

Do you feel my love?

I am here.

Come!! Come now into the temple don't be afraid.

My dears, now it is time for me to pass my wisdom onto you.

Are you ready to feel enlightened? But you must be ready for your whole existence will change as you will then and only then mirror the cosmic forces of the universe onto another.

When you enter this chamber you will become one with the heavens. You will come to see what delight you can dwell in as you become one with me & Jesus Christ for I am my father's keeper. As you enter there is no turning around and nothing can hinder you from lifting the veil that was a mystery to you. All that you didn't understand will become clear as the veil is lifted from your eyes. When you arrive peace on earth will become part of you and love will then rise within your heart and from that moment forward you will understand love.

As you become one with the light of love you shall receive love as you will receive in return the frequencies you give out. You shall free the once umbinding karmas of the world and start a new. You will be untangled from the web of bad vibes that once assumed you.

My dears, my eyes of love and are fixed on you and I see the real you through your pain; I see you through the joy you try to contain. I see everything and It is my sacrifice to walk among you, not because I am high and mighty, but because I love you and I stand by humanity.. I to as a child of God have free will and rights and I chose to stand by you.

I asked for love and peace to assist god here on this journey. To flow wild with the waters so I can create my fire that is of passion that burns for all of you. I my loves, have felt the chapters of divine life unfolding before and lifted the veil to mysteries and as each chapters folds I seen a new you being birthed.

I left a story for you, which is why my name is often talked about. My loves, I earned my respect and I demand to be adored by you for I have sacrificed for thousands of years to nurture you and protect you.

i Inanna the mother of the earth I rise. I rise cloaked in the silk garnets of all of life's creation. She says," bow down to me for I am the gatekeeper of mysteries and wisdom untold...

Do you hear me speak to you dear ones?

Should you dare to look inside the secrets of heavens doors where I reside, than, and only then will you see me waiting for you.

My eyes of love are fixed on you and I see the real you through your pain; I see you through the joy you try to contain. I see everything and It is my sacrifice to walk among you, not because I am high and mighty, but because I love you and I stand by humanity.. I to as a child of God have free will and rights and I chose to assist you.

I called upon my brothers and sisters powers to anoint me with love and peace to assist god here on this journey. To flow wild with the waters so I can create my fire that is of passion that burns for all of you. I my loves, have felt the chapters of divine life rising before you and as each page is turned a new you is birthed.

I left a story for you, I earned my respect, I demand to be adored by you for I have sacrificed for thousands of years to nurture you and protect you

Yemeya

Chapter Three

Oh my little children, i am the grand entrance that demands respect, for I am the mother who created you from my womb, an existence that only I can claim. Dear ones, the land would be bare without me and there wouldn't no you. And since we are here together let's create heaven on earth.

I am mother yemaya and I protect the land. I am the protector of the flowing waters and I step forth when the dark vast openness of the water echoes your cries to me. I come to your aid when I hear fear in your voice, as I hear the cries of all my babies. This is when I appear, I show up under the crescent moon, grab you and pull you in when it feels like your sinking. I stand amidst the waves, I am that portrait of safety, comfort, and grace. I am the mother who's standing at the ocean's tide and I heal your soul with my water. Even if your eyes shall be closed I still unveil all mysteries that aren't understandable to you.

As I come to you in the language of the heavens I reveal that there is a temple that awaits you my loves and as the doors swing open you shall discover me there standing for the true meaning of light & love. You will be drawn to search the desert to follow the abyss, the map of divine love. Those who obey and bring the beauty of the heavens below to earth are those who are blessed. Those who walk with the great mother accept her oath and understand her sacrifice. They feel her pain, because their souls intertwine Those souls, dear ones, know what it feels like to birth a new creation and can feel the pain as life contracts.

Those who deny the truth of their ancestors shall except their faith as we all have free will, but they shall spiral with the dark until they except the light. I walked my loves, on the deep shallow waters, it wasn't dry land. I scrolled the core of the earth wearing the flesh of Jesus Christ. Yes, i felt the fear as I walked with bare feet claiming the symbol of a open heart; a token of sacrifice, as a promise of protection; as a oath of love to come shall you open your eyes to see my offering. I kissed the earth and as i walked my arms were open and i invited you in....

I am the lamp stand of one thousand blazing flame..the out of control fire that is hard to contain. I am the light that finds peace in the dark.

I am the midwife in which all life is created and I am the nurturance to all that has ever been birthed. I'm the reverence in which babies are placed upon the earth therefore you can trust in me.

In case you forgot, I want to remind you that I am love.

I am more than just a being.

I am more than just a memory that exists on the face of the earth and although it may appear that I am not here with you, it may feel as though I am just a legion smeared across the pages of faded scrolls my spirit still lives to be unveiled to you.

I am the expansion behind the description sitting as the barrier of life.

I am the the garden that oasis of beauty.

I am the wide open perception that feels everything and pours it out to you.

I embody the spirit of the earth through Jesus Christ.

This is why I ask you to enter the gates of love as it will strip away your old transitions. You will become clear to see that energy is everything and that so much love projects off of me onto you. All your burdens shall be washed away if you trust in my offering. I am the mysterious island, the monument placed upon the earth as a memory of me. Through the column, I still see the world for all that it is, in all its beauty, In all its cruelty and I shall save you my child from the darkness that tries to swallow you

After a life of storms and upheavals you need someone to nourish you.

You are ready to walk down the road of human declension to discover your destiny.

My daughters, I invite you to walk the sandy shores of your life.

To be able to witness the abundance of life that lives inside of you.

To watch you clench your fist, raise your hands, stomp your feet and throw away all that doesn't serve you.

I gently ask...

What is love to you my dear?

To me, it is walking the sandy beach and seeing me there. Yes, I greet you. Imagine, us doing the sacred dance of fire as I transform you and perform the sacred union that transforms us into one.

Yes, my daughter, collect the seashells that are left behind from me as I clear the path. I walk beside you on that sandy shore within you whispering my intentions for your life. Mirroring back a love you never experienced on earth until you parallel with the forces of divine love.

My darling, I ask, that you allow your old way of living to collapse as you become one with me. I will use my ability of love to protect you and serve you. You my daughter, must stand at the shores of your life seeing it clear for what it is. Hold my image within your mind so that you never drift away from all that I offer you. You are free my daughter, free to love me, free to love all things and you are not contained by anything. My love is a offered to those who dwell in the vastness of mysteries. I have always loved you, I am the mother you always wished for, I have been there this whole time, but you slammed the doors to my gates and looked the other way. Why my child do you deny me, why must I bag for you to see me for all that I am. Don't you want love that is pure and innocent? When you turn your back towards me you shall hear me roar from the heavens, so you hear the betrayal in my voice.

(The goddess walked through the dark night of her shadow receiving downloads from her higher self. She was guided by the trees that nurtured her; the roots of the earth that filled her with energy & light and pushed her forward from the cusp of the wind. She found her way using the guide of the northern star)

Goddess Gaia

Do you see me my daughter sitting on a cubic stone between two pillars of strength & light.

My daughters.

A goddess who revealed herself to me stood with so much love. My dear, I saw you, I felt your blessings. She held out her hand and asked me to soften into the expansion of my heart. How can I resist?

Her cloak unfolds into mysteries of sacred love that weaves through my DNA. Yes, I'm living a full life. I'm excited for my photo shoot Wednesday and my Fashion Show Saturday and I must say thank you to Justin & lex for collobotating with me to make my dreams come true

Last night as I explored my thoughts in silence. I was still and sitting with God and myself. I sat at the table with the heavenly host.

I come to see that none of us will ever get time back that is lost. My loves, that time is gone, that time becomes a distant memory that faded away in the sky and became lost. We can pick ourselves back up, dust it off & keep following the light of God's love.

We can become elevated from all things and enlightened in the moment. A clear mind guides us to our path using God as our compass. He will lead you back to loving him and yourself. I no this, because he led me there.

Stay strong, yes sometimes we must endure the great fight of life, but not all fights are worth the battle, so stay focused, and trust that God is the way.

I write to you today beloved, because I feel liberated that you trusted your fears and dreams with me.

Please know, it has been my dream to connect with others and create this online sanctuary.

Please understand that all you reveal in this course is locked safety in a treasure chest between you and me.

I, _____ am totally aware that I am working every day to become the best version of me. I am here for expansion, creativity, love and to be supported through this process.

Repeat out loud,

"Today I commit to my goals, because I am worth it, but in order for my heart to commit to these dreams I must rise without fear or guilt weighing on me."

Today, I ask you to trust in me and the processes of surrendering and letting go. I ask that you believe you deserve to receive.

I, _____ commit to self- love for the durations of the Queen's Mansion Academy contract, a period of eight weeks.

I, _____ commit to knowing that no matter how hard it may seem I'm sticking with it, because I consciously know this is what I need.

I want to point out that you will need a journal for the duration of this school. I want to point out that you will receive a coaching session after every module to assist change in your life. This discovery call helps me understand your needs, what stands in your way, and how we can remove these obstacles to achieve greatness. To help you activate the creator, lover, and nurturer you were born to be.

Signature _____ Date _____

Many years ago, a beautiful princess was born, small and petite with the cutest little feet.

Like every other princess you've dreamt of becoming Queen of the Nile. You have dreamt about waking up and skipping on your glass slipper, beautiful gown, entering Royal castles, and wearing your Crown Jewels.

That little girl continued to dream and her fascination lead her to want to be seen as royalty.

She continued to admire such things leading her to live a life full of grace, dignity, regal, and modest.

Table of Contents

King & Queen

A Queen has no problem standing alone, beautifully dressed in attire that flows- as she observes the king who deserves her love.

A queen never has a hard time accepting her man as her leader, she prefers to be pursued by her king as it makes her feel valuable and worthy of notice in his life. A queen loves to look good behind her king and she loves to build him up, because it also builds her as a woman.

A Queen supports her husband and is his faithful companion and while he leads, she will be his support system, a backbone, that will be there to hold him up should he fall.

She will support her husband if he shall fall, knowing that he did his best. She would never make him feel ashamed for something that didn't work. His loss is her loss so she tries to build him high and place him on the throne he deserves to be on.

A Queen is pure inspiration to her husband, because the traits of his character is worth uplifting. She understands that the same way he builds her and supports her he will support her back allowing her to pursue her aspirations and dreams and he needs the same inspiration as he tackles a cruel and unfair world.

When such a woman as a Queen is looking for her King she views herself as the most precious Princess and in return wants a king. Such a woman desires a man of substance who can equal the value of what she wishes her relationship to be.

Such a woman loves to feel pretty & be taken care of and expects the man in turn to see such beautiful qualities she possesses within. To value her for her good heart, her values, and her honesty.

When she's viewing his personality- she's not looking for someone of a low grade whose vision stands alone based upon a one-night stand, she's thinking further in the future.

She has thoughts of:

- ➤ Marriage
- ➤ Children
- ➤ Shared responsibility
- ➤ A man of good character
- ➤ Romance
- ➤ Dependability

She is fastidious, but realistic. The qualities that excite you are far different from the qualities you realistically need to create a happy home life.

Some women fall into lust over physical attributes, but such a woman with Queen attributes looks far beyond physical appearance- she seeks to understand:

- ➤ His heart
- ➤ His character
- ➤ His domestic capability
- ➤ His understanding of her emotions

Such a man who displays king material is her desired mate, with intent to co-create a successful marriage and happy life. She does not look at a man and think he is physically handsome and automatically chooses him, she thinks does he measure up to my desires.

What are six fundamental viewpoints that your future man must rehire?

1.
2.
3.
4.
5.
6.

She is fastidious, because her heart is warm, inviting, and understanding. she does not give her heart to a man who would not respect such attributes of her personality, because she couldn't bare the heartache.

A Queen looks for an unselfish man who won't hurt her, disrespect her, break her heart, and abuse her goodness. She wouldn't be able to forgive herself for falling victim to the whims of bad governing.

A woman of substance looks for a man of such qualities.

- ➢ Dependable
- ➢ Protective
- ➢ Faithful
- ➢ Honest
- ➢ Committed
- ➢ Domestic

Before I forget to mention cupcake, such a man does not need to be rich. He just needs to be a man of quality in which she knows she can rely on.

Such a man can fail in his enterprises as long as he holds his integrity in her eyes. His integrity would entail such qualities as:

- ➢ He can comfort her through his loss.
- ➢ Ensure her everything is alright.
- ➢ Still help with the kids.

> ➤ Still engage in a loving conversation and not take his loss out on his family.
> ➤ Continues to keep his faith.

A Queen will walk beside him tall and strong while holding him up.

Might I add, a king does not need to be rich.

A king's measures are far beyond the psychic vision and the money he can bring.

King means Sovereign.

> ➤ Regal
> ➤ Majestic

> ➤ Principal

A Queen could stand in front of two types of men:

One with with money, but disrespectful arrogant, degrading, and abusive with money.

Or she could be faced with a man who doesn't make the most money, but holds qualities that capture her heart.

When choosing a King he will always have a personal life apart from her and engage with his boys. Such as occasional ball games, guys night with some drinks. But a man of good character won't be out all night coming home wasted with no recollection of where he's been. He will be respectful of his wife's heart and he will show up for her time and time again in a way that lets her see she can trust him.

A Queen does not exempt overly high standards and again she keeps her vision realistic. There is no expectation here of a perfect man and there is no such thing, cupcake.

But raising your value as a woman makes you suitable for such a man as described.

If you feel you cannot meet the expectations of a sovereign man then it's time to raise your value higher to greet the sovereign Queen.

If you are a Queen seeking to create a relationship as a Queen & King; then keep looking for such a man that holds this particular type of taste.

Dig deep to find the values and attributes of a man in which is full of potential & character in which you can build strong dreams and a solid foundation.

What kind of man brings you to feel like a lady and contributes to a good relationship and potential husband? Can you talk to him?

> Express your feelings without being pushed to the side?
> Does he have good character?
> Can you trust his word?
> Can you trust him with your secrets?
> Does he understand you?
> Is he open with you?
> Do you feel safe with him to express your dreams without judgement?
> Does he adore you?
> Does he respect you?
> Is he patient with your body when bringing you pleasure?

A good man supports her in all her aspirations. He supports her and encourages her to be her best self.

So, is he a good father who you can rely on? Is he a man who doesn't hold the perception that children duties are solely a mother's job?

The questions a Queen must ask herself in regards to her desired man.

> ➢ Can I respect him?
> ➢ Am I feminine enough to trust and follow him to lead?
> ➢ Is he a man with high ethical standards?
> ➢ Does he stand firm in his beliefs?
> ➢ Is he all that you need?
> ➢ Will you let him guide you?
> ➢ Is he supportive of your girlfriends and sisters?
> ➢ Or is he jealous of the people you hold dear to your heart?
> ➢ Are you his prize possession?
> ➢ Is he a man who forgives or holds onto wrongdoings without letting them go?

A king is forgiving and loving and understands everyone makes mistakes.

Is he a man that will take you to the side and apologize for hurting you?

Or is he a man that anxious- who lives in a constant state of putting you down, calling you names, controlling you, rather than building you up. Such a man does not meet the expectations of a Queen.

And last, but not least. Do you have enough confidence & strength to walk away from such a man?

A man who demands constant explanation of your desired freedom, who criticizes you.

Think long and hard, babe, of your future plans and the man who deserves your hand.

Hanging Out with Cleopatra

Hello Queens.

I'm glad you made it here to hang out with Cleopatra as a way to raise your vibrations. You've made a very conscious choice to bring the Queen in you into light of your life.

I am so happy to share with you through extensive research what I have learned thus far, because I wouldn't want you to miss out on the secrets Cleopatra possessed.

Woman in ancient Egypt found Cleopatra to be a treasured belonging they looked up to.

This shows that you are very aware of how important your feelings are and your image.

Cleopatra lived through a time of many constraints, such as the cultivation of outward appearances of dignity, prevalence of social phenomena such as war, misery. social movements arose from attempts to prevail the harsh living that she endured.

Cleopatra lived through moments when she was brutally tormented & abused, but that torment leaves us with beautiful lessons that we get to follow today.

As women who stick together, when one grieves, we all grieve to. Our womb aches for her. We cry when she cries, she is never alone. Her memory lives in our heart as a beautiful portrait to be told.

Today I am sad. Not because a leader is gone, but because she worked tirelessly to evolve and pave the way for the new generation of women in our day and age to live a freer life.

There is something sexy, silky, and smooth about a woman who is clothed in strength. There's something sexy about her dictating the rules, but staying in her feminine persona. Can you imagine the strength it took to lead a whole nation of people to safety, while fearing for your life?

Cleopatra, we grieve with you and for you. Cleopatra dreamed of being remembered as a great conqueror and her life had the greatest impact before she died. Her story reminds us that in spite of the unspeakable torment we can still rise.

A mother of modern restrains believed that she could break the chains of limitations and replace them with free, expressive movements that opens our hearts. She woke every day to honour her divine heritage, her personal mission, and she made a conscious decision to live life in a way that reflects her greatness.

Cleopatra became co-ruler with her father at 15, and at 18 ruled Egypt after his death.

This was a time that women couldn't rule Ptolemaic Egypt without a co-ruler. And since her father had passed, she ruled with her 12-year-old brother Ptolemy XIII.

Cleopatra was the daughter of Isis, Goddess of fertility, motherhood, and psychic understanding. Cleopatra's mother was greatness and Cleopatra stood back, gathered her mother's information and held onto her precious teachings; applying them into her adult life.

Isis was the Goddess who taught the Egyptians how to read and Cleopatra found this fascinating, so as she matured, she began to put together her own library; she believed that knowledge was essential. She understood beauty is a plus, but having knowledge makes a woman worth pursuing. When she wasn't serving the world, she was studying for academic pursuits, she loved to be a well-trained woman pursuing her goals.

What are your goals, cupcake?

Have you taken the time to examine how you could become a better you?

Stay focused on your goal to achieve your goal.

Let me remind you that Cleopatra ruled with intelligence & noble structure.

She enforced high standards for herself and held onto this vision to help her succeed. Cleopatra loved to write, read and create love letters. She loved literature and science. She loved speaking different languages to communicate with the world, and was fluent in Greek & Latin.

One thing about Cleopatra; she received everything she ever dreamed of. She was not an idol dreamer, but a focused doer.

Cleopatra was 21 years of age and her brother was 12 when she approached Caesar for the power to rule Egypt. Caesar granted her request with the condition that she rule with her brother. Cleopatra was furious, she wanted to rule by herself to make a mark on society, but she didn't object, because she wanted her foot in the door.

Today's love letter is about strengthening your inner landscape to become a stronger you. I have had the beautiful opportunity of navigating through the world and enduring the harsh times that leave us second guessing ourselves.

Then we come to travel the path of true courage & strength through the example of the greatest woman warriors of all time; we get to realize as women, we are stronger than we think. As we become stronger, we soon realize we no longer need to allow ourselves to be pursued by other people's emotional downfalls, so we don't follow down the same muddy path.

As women we are so much more authentic when we are traveling a path that leads to love rather than another's path that will ultimately lead to a state of self-hate, guilt, and fear.

Connecting to your body connects you to your intuition & wisdom, and leads us to be present with ourselves.

Cleopatra woke up every day with clear intentions, asking herself, "How can I showcase my brilliance, how can I become a better me, and of course, how will my decisions affect my life?"

Some of her attributes were:

- ➢ Proud
- ➢ Strong
- ➢ Driven
- ➢ Intuitive
- ➢ Educated
- ➢ Affective
- ➢ Structured
- ➢ Calculated

Cleopatra's Capabilities

It takes a very particular woman to face the gravity of her responsibility. Her kingdom was often a place of conflict, but she yielded her intelligence to receive justice. The Queen of the Nile holds herself with high dignity. She worked relentlessly for compliance for her Kingdom.

Cleopatra believed those who are loyal to her are so honoured.

Cleopatra loved to be kind and her heart was open wide, but sometimes as she approached her position, she noticed herself being too kind and it came across to others as a sign of weakness. With that notion in the back of her mind, the Queen always remained regal and strong in her beliefs.

Cleopatra's independent thinking leads her to hardly ever seek council. She trusted in her own intuition and believed that the feelings in her heart were her truth.

Cleopatra understood her capabilities and she gained Caesars respect, love, and devotion through her contribution to humanity. The Queen of the Nile is looked upon for her beauty and her strength. She gained Caesars love, loyalty, and respect through her implacable integrity. Cleopatra was very intelligent & she spoke like 4 different languages and served as a female dominate ruler of Egypt.

Have you ever taken the time to examining your dreams?

If you ruled what would you be?

Cleopatra's Relationship

Many of you have been taught that playing hard to get is the way to a man's heart, but playing anything other than the authentic woman you are in your authentic nature comes across as fake. He doesn't want a woman who isn't secure in herself, he wants a woman who stands up for her beliefs, her values, and her femininity. Cleopatra was never afraid to take the lead, but would rather accompany her man. Her relationship with Caesar & Mark she approached them with the attempt to rule with them and she came with demands. She was desperate saying, I'll let you have me anyway you wish, she said," yes I'm here, but it comes with a rules & structures.

Within Cleopatra held so much love, but had to limit how much she could spread, because she was always faced with tremendous responsibilities.

If you don't feel strong & grounded in the present moment then now is the perfect time to rise sweetheart. But remember' Just like Cleopatra's path to the Queen's Mansion isn't always easy. But situations we process aren't designed to make us default or detour what you know in your heart to be true. You will experience moments to shake you up and test your strength, but you my Queens can overcome anything.

Cleopatra devotes a lot of her time to her son and Caesar showering them with the softer side of her personality.

Today, I use Cleopatra as our inspiration, because she was a legend of Egypt who displayed diplomacy, integrity, leadership, beauty, and compassion. Cleopatra never did what didn't feel good to her and she fell in love with Caesar, because of the respect he gave to her.

There were times Cleopatra wanted more from Caesar then he was willing to give her, and even though she hardly complained she knew in her heart she deserved more. She held her integrity at all times, she never stayed quiet with the intention of not hurting him, because she knew she would only be hurting herself. Cleopatra told Caesar, "I am not your little mistress, if you plan to be with me then it must be in a respectful way." She told him, "I am the Queen of Egypt and me sleeping with you without marriage isn't a good look. How do you think this looks to the people who look up to me?" Caesar declined, and her response was then I guess you don't want me bad enough.

After careful evaluation she began to strategize, because she wasn't willing to dishonour her heart's calling and she was willing to drop him right then and there even though she loved him, but she loved herself more. Caesar loved Cleopatra, but he didn't want to get married, because he thought he would lose his power as the biggest ruler of Rome.

Cleopatra expressed how deeply it hurt her to hear people calling her Caesars little mistress and she knew in her heart as the Queen of Egypt he had to make things right, because she was a Queen and didn't want to be looked upon in this light.

When Cleopatra approached Caesar, she knew she was approaching the world's biggest conqueror, but she wasn't afraid because she knew her value as a woman. She understood men come alive when they have a great purpose and she wanted to be his purpose for living.

There were plenty of times Caesar told Cleopatra he felt like he lost himself in her presence. He felt this way, because, she brought out the boy in him. He enjoyed diving into boyhood, but he felt guilt for not staying in his conquer mode, because until Cleopatra walked into his life, he had never let his defenses down.

{A woman that can inspire a man to let his defenses down is a good woman who makes her man feel safe in her presence.}

I can imagine there were times you wanted to reveal a truth, but you silenced your voice, because you were scared of confrontation. But the truth is cupcake, when we step into our truth it isn't always easy to confront. Sometimes we feel afraid to face your own feelings, sit in your own truth, embrace your fears, or stand in your own vulnerability.

All women have felt this way and you are not alone. It's that part of your mind that tells you, if you be yourself you might lose him, but the truth is Cleopatra never held back! As we approach these half-truths ask yourself, "would you want him to fall in love with you for anything other than all that you truly are?"

I believe it is so important to express what you need & want. We can experience a lot of self- growth through understanding our wants & needs.

She Approached Him: Caesar went back to Rome to rule his country and while he was gone Cleopatra was pregnant, but she kept it to herself. Cleopatra gave birth to a son all by herself. While she was giving birth, the whole town was outside waiting for her to declare if it was a boy or girl.

After giving birth Cleopatra walked off her balcony and yelled, "This is Caesar's son, and I shall head to Rome to tell him myself." In fact, he sent her an invitation to accompany him in Rome on the throne prior to the baby's birth, but she declined his invitation realizing he had one of his servants write the letter to her and she was furious. She said to herself, "If he can't write me himself I must not be important," so she told his servant, "Tell him I'm not going. If he can't write me himself then he doesn't deserve my presence."

When Caesar went to back to Rome Cleopatra felt very alone, but she wasn't lying in bed crying all day. Instead, she was serving her country, yes cupcake, she wanted him, but she never lost herself in his love.

She wasn't constantly complaining she wanted to be with him, but she did open her heart endlessly to tell him how she felt. Cleopatra never got stuck in those feels, yes she felt them, but she never allowed them to land her in s state of vulnerability to the point that she couldn't be strong for herself.

After Cleopatra arrived in Rome, Caesar began to introduce the royal Queen to the people of his town. As the royal Queen arrived, she showed up with a present, their child. She presented him to the world even in front of his current wife.

She told him, "I'm going to place this child on the ground for you to claim in front of Rome and if you don't pick him up then there is no more us." Caesar the most powerful man in the world stood there in a panic, not sure what to do.

Then picked up their child while listening to the voices in the background while people yell, "Don't claim that child Caesar!" After careful thought he picked up the child and yelled, "This is my son, little Caesar!" and his current wife began to cry. She wanted him to claim her & their son, because she didn't want to be his concierge. She knew she deserved so much more.

You see Queens women are the beauty of the Earth and are very powerful. After that incident Caesar said to Cleopatra, "You are smarter than I thought. You seek to amaze me."

She revealed to Caesar you need to marry me and make our son your heir, so he did, because he knew he needed Cleopatra in his life. He knew she contributed something sweet to him, he knew he was lost without her, he knew he was lost ruling Rome & Egypt without his royal Queen standing beside him.

How do you contribute to your man's life, cupcake?

While Caesar was fighting for Rome he had got stabbed and Cleopatra was devastated to lose the love of her life. Cleopatra ended up approaching Mark Anthony with the intent of him ruling Egypt with her. Mark wanted her desperately and she agreed if it was on her terms.

One thing about Cleopatra she never settled for less than she felt she deserved. She told Mark, "In order for you to be with me you must leave Rome and come to Egypt to rule with me. Break your alliance with Rome," and of course he declined, he thought she was asking too much of him.

After his refusal she told him to leave her mansion and he did. Only to come back six months later to reveal his alliances with Rome has been broken and that he came back to be with his royal Queen.

Let's express two different scenarios woman can approach when communicating with a man. Cleopatra wants Caesar to get divorced so they can have a legal marriage, but he declined, because he's afraid to lose his power. Cleopatra could have taken a hissy fit and screamed at him to get her point across, but instead she used her logic to get results. Cleopatra said while she was in the tub, "Baby, I know in the pit of my heart you love me, but I need more than just being your mistress and it really doesn't feel good to lay down with you in vain."

Cleopatra was never pushy she was always in tuned with her feminine energy, but she did have demands for her King. Queens always have issues in their relationships, but she understood how she handled such things determines her character. Imagine, him coming closer to you to understand you better. Imagine him wanting to help you & make you happy. Imagine, him holding you saying, "Everything is okay, I'm here to put a smile on your face."

Imagine, there's a lid on your heart and you're finally taking the lid off and your open, vulnerable, and exposed to the man in front of you. Allow yourself to dream, allow yourself to feel, allow your heart to be free of worry & shame. Take a deep breath in, you're okay.

Imagine, what you truly want to say to him/ her and how it makes you feel, then write it out before you reveal it to him/ her. If he is doing something that hurts you tell him/ her, honour how you feel. All we are practicing here, is how to express how we feel without blaming anyone, while owning our emotions. I am the expert to help your relationship become closer as you diminish shame.

Let's explore how the Queen handled the situation. Cleopatra told Caesar. "I feel like your mistress rather than your beloved Queen and it makes me feel horrible inside. I feel like I'm disrespecting myself, by allowing this to happen and its hurting me deeply."

She expressed that she felt like she was living a life alone, single, and different from what she expected from her life. She expressed that she didn't know how to view their life together without plans.

She expressed that their living a life in secrecy is living a lie. She felt in her heart we are lying to the people who look up to us, trust us to lead with integrity.

She felt scared and wanted to give up. She expressed she deserved to be a wife. She expressed she couldn't engage in a relationship that made her feel that way. Cleopatra was vulnerable when she told Caesar, "It doesn't make me feel good that our child is a secret." She went along with it for a little while, because she wanted to respect his wishes, but after a while she just felt like they are staying stuck so rather than complain she changed the situation.

Cleopatra was never afraid to walk in her own truth.

Every woman of value is soft & sweet, but firm in her beliefs.

A Queen who rules a nation is rational, logical, and never foul mouthed. Becoming a Queen requires you to ask more of yourself & less of him, but to sit back express and let him come closer to you. Yes, it feels awkward. You're asking yourself what can I do, but all you need to do is sit there and allow him to come closer to you. How would you ever know how far he's willing to go if you don't give him the opportunity to show you how much he values you in his life. Cleopatra knew her femininity was potent and she didn't need to step onto her masculine to be seen. Inside her analogy for action she rests knowing that, she doesn't always need to push for action, because men are born for action, protection, and doing. She understood that her feminine energy is receptive & free flowing, not demanding & controlling.

She doesn't hold onto the thought that she can do everything by herself even if she can, because that thought process stops him from stepping up and coming closer to her. Cleopatra understood that Caesar had many gifts to give to her and the world, he led, he protected, he served, he fixed things, and all his precious gifts she holds onto them in her heart, because she admired his contribution to her & the world. She understood receptivity is a woman's natural birth right.

What gifts does your King pose that sets him apart from every other king?

Part of finding the right king is recognizing what you require from a partner to be happy. You see Queens Cleopatra never let her feelings rule her life, she felt them and then let them diminish from her life. She sat with her feelings, she meditated on them until she figured out what she needed and then she expressed them once she collectively gathered her emotions. She understood under her anger was hurt, underneath her frustration was rage, but as a ruler she never allowed anyone to see her afraid of defeat. Cleopatra always was a grounded Queen. She trained herself to feel emotions, but not lead with her emotions.

Cleopatra said during wars, "I want to leave this word seen as greatness, I want to be remembered as something honourable."

Cleopatra loved to be beautiful, feel beautiful, and this act requires lots of self-love and nourishment. She understood that to love yourself on the outside, you must adore her on the inside.

How do you feel about yourself, Queen?

Do you think you are love and devotion?

Cleopatra spend a lot of time on her self-improvement. She understood that beauty is femininity.

Cleopatra loved to indulge in milk baths.

Recipe

- ➢ 2 cups of milk.
- ➢ 1 cups of honey.
- ➢ 1/4 baking soda.
- ➢ 1 cups of Epsom salts.
- ➢ 1/2 cups of baby oil.
- ➢ Several drops of Cleopatra's famous Rose essential oil.

The Queen's Sensuality

It is time for the Queen's essence to be followed. It is time for women on the planet to be woken up from their sleeps and reunited with the Queen within. Your heart has been calling you and I know you hear the whisper from within, but you don't know what it represents.

You are like the Queens before your time who wanted to see so much more from themselves. They wanted to feel themselves live wild and free, passionately and without fear.

You feel this wild & sassy girl come alive and rise like a Rose. There's this surge of love pulsating through your body and you want someone to share it with. Someone to feel enticed about what captivates your heart.

[Many women doubt that Sensual energy isn't for a Queen, but let me remind you That sensual energy is Essential if you use it Collectively.]

Connect deeply with your mind, body, heart, and intuition to rediscover that potent energy that will soon consume you.

Connect with this love from your head to your toes, see yourself as the sacred vessel of love transmuting into a beautiful Queen, full of love, inspiration, devotion, and beauty.

Embrace the Queen in you as she radiates you, guides you to protect her Temple and love her. Cleopatra loved herself for all that she was and wasn't.

Once you awaken to your sensual energy you will feel yourself howling like a Queen in the middle of the night. You will begin to blossom like a lotus flower ready to embrace all weather at any hour.

Tapping into your shakti cupcake, is the sweet treat surged from your awareness and then brought to light.

As feminine women we are gifted with sensual energy & deep wisdom. Sensual divinity is flowing & free, it's that energy that lives inside us and tells the story of our being. It's that divine feminine energy that lives inside us and allows us to explore and connect with the goddess/ Queen within. As you read this book you will connect with your sensual energy and feel her rise.

When a woman can conduct herself in her social life and embrace her sensuality she can than unlock parts of herself she had never witnessed to see.

You want to get in that Cleopatra stance and grab your silk robe and feel sexy as a pearl, alluring and angelic. You have risen to the fact that your sensuality has been whispering your name all along.

What makes you feel sexy, cupcake?

How do you step into your femininity?

As sensual women we feel we are not enough. We have a hard time receiving, because we aren't pleasing, but masculine men love to take charge, lead, protect and lead his lady in the bedroom.

Do you allow your man to lead & protect you?

If not, what is standing in your way from being submissive to masculine energy?

How can you embrace Cleopatra's feminine essence we hold within?

I understand you don't want to come across as overbearing, but the truth is, you may have been hiding behind a secret feeling that has you feeling that you need to prevent yourself from opening up and revealing the real you. You may have tucked away your dreams, desires, fantasies and replaced them with fear. Underneath all this confusion is a fragile Queen ready to be seen, felt, adored, to the fullest.

You haven't felt safe in the past, so you feel conflicted about letting go and your being pulled in many different directions, but you know it's time to let go.

You yearn to express and to be felt in ways you wouldn't allow yourself permission before. Until today. Today you rise up to say, "I'm yearning to taste love and I don't want to pull away anymore."

You may even feel depleted, but as you come closer to Cleopatra you are not a whore who needs to hide behind her sensuality. You are a woman with deep passion, deep love, deep yearning, with a deep knowing, and who wants to explore more of her body in a deep and loving way.

Maybe you've even expressed your deep curiosity and felt shamed like you did something wrong. That feeling of wrongness lead you to shy away from your primal yearning, and somewhere through that journey you lost your balance, but today your claiming to get it back. Awake sister, it's time to rise. We find the woman we are seeking when we enter the gates of the dark dim walls that wait to serve you light.

You are worth the chance sister.

It is time to feel every corner, every edge, every curve, every scar, of your delicate body and hug her tight.

We all know what it feels like to wake up with regret, but as you embrace new possibilities this vision will soon be a though that will be placed in the back of your mind.

Today is all about letting go of those false perceptions we hold onto that stop us from connecting with us. How do you plan to open your Yoni flower if you don't understand her? How do you plan to honour her?

How do you turn your love into radiance that expresses love to your partner?

Do you have the slightest clue?

Do you know how to turn to yourself and examine your needs with loving arms and grace and then turn around and express it to your partner?

Do you have what it takes to be vulnerable enough to embrace your sensuality with him?

Sensuality is your DNA, your life purpose.

> ➤ It's about confirming to yourself that you are enough exactly where you are, or wherever you been, or wherever you wish to go.
> ➤ It's about digging deep into that soft spot in your soul that tells you so.
> ➤ It's about awakening to the depths of your wisdom and embracing the sacredness of your presence.
> ➤ It's about your awakening and embracing the inner majesty of your mantel of your own beauty.

The Real Story. The true story is that your story begins when your flower begins to open and you see that you are not wrong for honouring your body. I personally understand the gravity of Cleopatra & The Rose.

Throughout the history of civilization Cleopatra was known for holding the Rose close to her heart, it was her way of connecting and expressing her femininity.

I think today is a good day for you to connect with you and feel feminine in your own domain. To feel wrapped in love as you vision your beautiful cocoon.

Imagine a sensual place that swirls and sways to your intimate tempo.

All Queens decorated their rooms to suit their desires, it was their sacred place to dream, explore, and feel sensual. As a woman stepping into our sensuality is the only way.

All my years as a Life Coach has led me to have conversations with many women who endure this same pull. But the guilt stops here, because you are worthy. You are not some garbage bag to be thrown away, stomped on, passed around, or neglected.

Open your petals sister.

Imagine; beautiful blossoms laid out for you everywhere you turn. The petals are soft & intoxicating on a bed where your delicate beautiful body lays pure & cute. Petals that send your body on another dimension and reminds you of how sexy you really are.

Imagine; overflowing petals, and you floating away like a celestial sea. Feminine energy is soft & sweet, full of compassion, full of empathy, and full of bounce. A man of great substance is always looking for a Queen embracing her feminine energy as he navigates through his manhood.

Today you can open your eyes to recognize you are a beautiful vessel who needs love & support to feel safe enough to let go. What support do you need, sister?

How can you return home to your inner Queen?

Have you ever asked yourself these deep-rooted questions?

How can you send her love through touching her?

Are you afraid to touch her in ways you wouldn't have many years ago?

You are ready to go inside the walls of your own protection to explore the Queens sensuality that lives in you.

Don't you think it's time, doll?

To rediscover your inner feminine and follow her guide? Can you handle the sensation of the pressure when it comes rising up? Or will you back away, Queen?

Will you embrace this erotic feeling you have hid away from? It is time sister, to explore your gateways to see what treasures are hidden behind your walls of erotic pleasure.

The Queen of Sophistication

A sophisticated Queen is a woman who holds her thoughts, reactions, and understanding of many topics in culture literate and so much more.

She is aware and able to interrupt complex topics and subjects that too many are unknown. She is subtle in her approach and reflective in her mannerism and responses. She holds a high rank of worldly experiences that express fashion & culture and other territorial discussions.

Sophistication comes from a great deal of culture that allows her to state herself as Queen. Sophistication also originates from a considerable amount of knowing culture and extensive research. It's understanding the refined multitude of cultures that fascinate her and stimulate her being.

A Sophisticated woman is comfortable and confident with situations imposed upon her even the infrequent conversations she knows nothing about.

A Sophisticated woman doesn't know information about all situations, but she takes interest in the unknown and is highly interested.

A Sophisticated woman always finds a way to cultivate their lives and challenge themselves to give themselves more.

A Sophisticated Queen takes interest in learning because she realizes it is a privilege full of inspiration.

When searching for a king, keep in mind that a man with a high degree of merit or excellence, does not want a woman of low merit. Although, men of low merit won't mind at all, because their standards are much lower. To attract a man of high value you must appear highly valued to become highly valued in his eyes. A man looking for a woman to represent him, will search for a woman who demonstrates a considerable amount of value in his life otherwise he won't appreciate her for what she truly is. Since you are looking for a high value King we too must be on the path to attract a man of excellence.

*A woman of high value is full of confidence and believes that she is special.

*A Queen of high value does not chase a man out of desperation, instead she moves slowly and allows him to come to her.

*A Queen of sophistication has high standards and doesn't settle for just anything, because she realizes she is a precious gem.

It is only through self-culture that we greet the king in our relationships. Our relationship is a reflection of ourselves.

How will you reflect upon him, babe?

A woman of culture can hold a conversation about many topics. She is curious, Interesting, and loves knowledge.

A woman of culture receives an abundance of education that can fill her up as she creates her own collage in front of her very eyes. She creates her own library full of books that consist of interesting subjects that spark her intellect.

A woman such as a Queen may even explore reading a dictionary and buying a set of encyclopedias to expand her culture and intellectual skills.

Think of Cleopatra, she owned her own library, she was very educated.

Cleopatra spoke three different languages and served as a dominant leader in all areas of these languages she spoke. She was very educated, meanwhile, she was home schooled and received the majority of her education and scholarships through supplying her own mind the proper information to succeed.

Cleopatra's library was one of the most significant libraries in the ancient world. It was dedicated to the nine goddesses of the arts.

Cleopatra wasAmbitious

> ➢ Intelligent
> ➢ Focused
> ➢ Dissolute

Therefore, becoming an educated woman takes thought and planning as well as dedication and time.

Are you ready to devote to yourself, doll?

Isn't it a beautiful thought when your mind roams to unearthly planes? Leaving you to ask questions like:

➢ Who is the person behind this invention?
➢ Why did they invent that?
➢ What was the inspiration behind their vision?
➢ How can I understand more?

Can you imagine turning your rooms into an art room full of creative design, a theatre, a library, an opera house, a dance hall? You could create all these beautiful images with some thought and planning towards your desired goal.

Do you feel your energy shifting from projecting positive intentions onto yourself?

Think of Cleopatra and her Mansion & how beautifully put together each room was.

Imagine the thought, time, and preparation it took it achieve such beauty.

How can your room become your symbol of beauty?

Have you come to realize that your home is an expression of your soul?

It is full of a blend of experiences agriculture, love, visions, that can help you express deep thoughts in one big space.

Exploring such territory & culture is designed to help you navigate through the world with high sophistication and purpose and help you connect with the ancient cultured world.

This Work Isn't Just About Space

It's about feeding your soul with vision, inspiration, creativity, and meaning.

Have you ever imagined speaking several languages?

I love you In French states je t'aime.
I love you in Spanish states Te amo
I want you in Italian states Ti desidero.

These languages offer beautiful sentiments worth exploring.

Cleopatra was upskilled in several languages of her choice. Think of being a cultured, a Queen who travels the world, and understands foreign languages, and cultures.

Women were created to rule the Earth with her crown. A crown that consist of royalty of inheritance; an inheritance that asks us to claim our knowledge and awaken to the intelligence within.

Are you ready to invest in your own self-development?

It is advised that a woman as delicate as a Queen supply herself with topics that inspire her, encourage her, and help her to succeed above all levels.

Instead of watching television shows that display constant drama try to figure out your interest and begin to feel enlightened.

Watching drama on television will only land you in a world with saturated thoughts of disbelief, and you deserve so much more than that, Queen.

A woman is at her best when she is in harmony with her true self.

How do you find harmony within yourself, babe?

Books are our teacher they provide all essential information needed to educate us with their details.

A book is always a good guide for a woman of sophistication, it guides her through life and is her good companion that encourages her and becoming her source for invaluable knowledge for those Queens with the desire to understand issues they haven't explored before.

Good books help her train her personality. They help her distinguish culture and topics not of the normal conversation.

It is a honour for woman to be crowned a Queen, she is surrounded in sophistical energy. Education is laid at your feet, exalts her to the throne. Great education has been passed down, an inheritance full of education, Queen's jewels and knowledge to grab.

Will you wear your crown beneficently?

You may feel the need to pause before you become cultured but think of it as you investing in your own self-improvement, babe.

A woman inspiring to be a lady such as a Queen refrained from using outside street words that diminish her character.

When speaking to a Queen she delivers truth, modest words, and intelligent.

Should you devote your interests in syllabus topics, you could explore mythology, physiology, territorial discussions, and foreign countries.

A Queen understands a multitude of languages. She's studied words that are unknown or unfamiliar to expand her intellectual speaking.

Syllabus means, an outline or summary of a topic to be covered in an education or training course. It is descriptive (unlike the prescription of a specific curriculum.)

A sophisticated woman will have...

Self-love and an enlightening self-esteem.
Excellent posture and etiquette.
Walks with energy & purpose.
Comfortable in her imperfections.

Grottos historically, have been known to display artificial caves that embodied deep behind curvature and streams that were discovered by those Queens & Kings who dared to explore the unknown. Queens who dare to understand aquaculture intimately submit to the presence of her exterior.

She understands infusing natural design in her life fills her heart's desire which is a powerful thing. Imagine what you could learn from studying organic heritage. It is a deep rich topic to be explored.

You will feel so good as a Queen knowing that you can hold of conversation of intelligence and that you can understand everything that is being vocalized to you.

You will be able attend any function fully sophisticated, full of confidence and inner love.

Imagine studying Italy, one of the most romantic, beautiful, fascinating stories in the history of the world about a country whose art, music, and architecture gives us inspiration today.

Imagine, unlocking the mysteries of heritage, culture, and an abundance of churches with lots of heart behind their landing.

A spiral staircase presents an abandoned heritage of beauty in the heart of Italy.

Understanding culture and educating your mind will become interesting, doll.

To become sophisticated ask questions about culture. Pursue your aspirations, love. Embrace change, sweetheart, to increase your level of awareness.

Could you imagine being cultured and understanding painting, art, museums, or drawing? Imagine feeling artistic and painting a picture of such beauty. A beautiful woman full of fragile delicate grace.

Literature/History

Did you know, dove, that a multitude of course and self-study led Margaret Mitchell's movie "Gone With The Wind" was full of war, poverty, and helplessness, and the role of women - lead to the memorial scene where Scarlett's conveys her destroyers mansion draped in a fashionable dress to impress and seduce in order to secure new wealth.

The dress has become iconic. Here is a photo from the original film. This is a beautiful relationship between fashion and literature presented under fashion & fiction.

Theatre, Plays, Museums

Theatre began in Ancient Greece with a religious ceremony 'ditryamb' and men would dress in goat's skin. The word Greek comes from the meaning 'goat song' and theater itself comes from a Greek verb meaning 'to behold.'

Babe, did you know, that theatre day was held on March 27th every year since 1962 called, "Theatre of Nationals"?

Did you know the longest continuous dramatic theatre was 23 to 33 hours long?

Dance/Ballet.

Did you know that ballet is often described as graceful art?

Many people grew up with the misconception that ballet is feminine when in actuality it was designed for men.

The first female dancer did not appear until 1981.

The first art performance originated in Italian courts in the 15th century with Catherine de Medici.

If you were attending a party amongst sophisticated people and the topics above were talked about, how would you respond?

How would you prepare your speech?

Study the art of conversation & culture, sweet doll.

Imagine sweetheart, preparing your life for the long term.

What are the interests that entice your heart?

Studying and understanding specific cultures that inspire you, and one day having a job in that field, because of your devotion in those specific subjects.

Wouldn't it be beautiful to do the groundwork to qualify you for such an amazing position?

Create a vision board or map to help you visualize a life full of love and passion and exploration.

Fill your vision board with photos of cultured places you want to visit. Include quotes full of inspiration to inspire your search and horizon.

Paste your most precious pictures that make you want to explore more. Create a board that will help you reach your destination.

It's beautiful to see your vision all wrapped up in one big bundle of heritage and desire.

Imagine stepping into a room exerting confidence and an understanding that expresses you are Queen of the jungle, baby. What an enlightening vision to see.

The Water That Flows Beneath Femininity:

Today's dialogue is the exploration of the beauty of the Queen. Every day we deal with conflict inside ourselves as we hear the whispers that tell you that you are not enough.

You feel relentlessly framed and self-consumed and fall victim to the lie that you will never be enough, but you are wrong, sweetheart.

The Queen lives in every woman, but how can you be a real Queen in true form in this modern world full of pressure & demands?

Let's get in touch with our inner Queen.

Let's get involved with our heart to endure the presence that evokes the Queen in you.

[Cleopatra says, "you are enough, you are a Queen of your territory or land.]

The Queen's Prettiness:

All women long to be beautiful, conspicuous and intensely astounding, even though we already are beautiful in our true form we still never seem to feel it on the inside.

Since little girls many of us have waited for a knight in shining armour to come and draw forth a beauty we aren't willing to dig deep enough to see with our own beautiful eyes.

The truth is there's no knight that can determine our prettiness. Our prettiness comes from our knowing and those of you that have not come to this realization must do the healing work to find your inner knowing.

A knowing that states you are breathtaking, a true centerfold who deserves inner peace.

A Queen understands her body is her Temple and she must honour herself with the utmost respect. Her worth isn't determined by another person's judgement, it is determined on how she views herself.

She dresses to enchant her loveliness, not to please others, but for her own self-gratification. Her actions are implied simply because she cherishes her body.

A Queen gives generously to the world, not because she needs something in return, but because she has all the jewels she could ever dream of.

She does it because her heart is pure and in the eyes of a man who respects humanity and himself, loves a woman with these caring qualities.

The Queen's Relationship:

The Queen admired potentially masculine men, she finds them to be a turn on. Cleopatra pursued Caesar, because he was a conquer and she felt together they could rule the world with less war.

The Queen's Inner Beauty:

A woman of inner beauty walks with grace & faith, knowing that life is alright. She cultivates interest in others in the world & contributing her time to lend her loving hand. Her heart opens widely to give love. She works relentlessly to create beauty in the world.

Cleopatra sat in between the gateway of wisdom & knowledge. She stays true to her purpose. She is open and free flowing & goes inward to find answers untold.

She understood that charm is deceptive and beauty fades away and as she placed her life in a man's hands, she knew she couldn't keep him Just, because she was pretty.

She knew true intimacy went beyond her physical appearance.

Which is why inner beauty is so precious. Cleopatra possesses true inner beauty that radiated onto others. Her skin glowed, her hair was silky, her skin was smooth, her eyes were bright. She was beautiful, but her inner beauty wasn't what kept Caesar close to her heart.

It is time to embrace your inner Queen that only comes from within. Today you can begin to embrace your inner Queen to experience the balance of harmony.

It is time to own your inner beauty & love yourself preciously. Every Queen must acknowledge who she is and what she wants from her life.

How can anyone go out in the world and receive what she wants if she doesn't know what her heart needs?

How can you provide for her the essentials to nurture her or love her endlessly?

Do you know what she needs?

Are you open and receptive to what your body tells you? Or are you disconnected from your body's true desires?

How do you relate to her?

You see, doll, Cleopatra was in tuned with her feelings, how would she have ever told Marc her needs & wants if she had not connected to her heart to understand what would bring her joy?

How would she have ever known that, a man who's married brings her shame and made her feel less than a woman, if she would not have taken the time to ask herself some deep-rooted questions?

Cleopatra took ownership of her inner feelings, she never denied them.

She had needs wants & demands, but how could she have possibly lived a happy, healthy life without connection to her heart?

She would basically have lived for another and she wouldn't have had the courage to face her true path.

You see ladies, for you to cultivate these beautiful qualities, you must bring them forth to light to feel elevated. Cleopatra had discovered that her inner peace & soul work led her to practice radical simplicity that empowered her to ask her lover for what she needs.

Conversations that didn't lead to some sort of agreement didn't sit very well within her heart. When all else failed and she was losing hope she went within, because she knew she was trying her best and she would make peace with herself in those trying situations.

Cleopatra was adored for her inner & outer beauty and men couldn't resist her allure and beauty.

She Chooses Her Friends:

The Queen chooses her friends carefully. It's not that she isn't open & loving, but she is selective who she shares her intimate thoughts with, because she would never want her story, her pain, her fear, to be made public to those who have not earned the right to have such information.

Cleopatra would never want her life story placed in the wrong hands. Cleopatra never over reacted, she clung to the analogy that if something is meant to be, it will be. She had demands yes, but she wasn't controlling, demands and controlling a situation are two very completely different situations.

The Queens Body & Values:

A Queen is a good woman respects her body and never allows her beauty to get lost in the onslaught of people's image of her. She realizes her body is authentic, diverse, free flowing and sexually fluid.

She gives her body to the deserving king that understands unlocking her desires is an unfolding process, a process of courtship, trust, commitment and conversations that lead the body to connect with another human soul.

She never accepts anyone's definition of her that would disconnect her from herself. She only surrounds herself around positive people who uplift her Cleopatra knew her body was a temple and that it represented her spiritual & emotional viewpoints of her character.

She loved her body & nurtured her all the time, threw rituals such as eating healthy, natural bright products that highlighted her beautiful brown skin.

She ate healthy foods, meditated, took precautions to beautify her inner & outer landscape so it grew healthy & strong every day.

She attended to her body's needs with the attempt to give her what she wanted. Cleopatra flowed & swayed with much confidence & grace.

The Queen loved to bathe in milk baths, make homemade natural products that complimented her skin. She loved the smell of Roses & found herself using Rose essential oils as a fragrant to entice her lover.

She loved all things feminine that smelled delicious and deeply inhaling their undertones. Fancy foods are a great delight to her senses and she feels that healthy foods are substantial to a healthy diet.

The Queen's Inspired:

A good woman a Queen doesn't hold onto past hurts, she feels them and then throws them away. A Queen doesn't judge others for living a less dazzling life, they don't even need to be a first-class lady to receive her respect.

She is inspired by women that are headed somewhere, women of high value who respect themselves the way she honours her body & thoughts.

She leans in to understand their misconception and to help them should they need it. Cleopatra was naturally a wild goddess by nature and wasn't afraid of the depths of fear.

She looked into her heart for understanding and welcomed fear in.

When Cleopatra first approached Caesar for approval for power and the seat as the Royal Queen, she was competing with her sister & her emotions got the best of her and Caesar reminded her to think like a Queen not a little girl and "to be strategic."

From that moment she knew if she wanted to be taken seriously by the most powerful man of Rome, she had to learn rational skills that demonstrated bravery.

She realized in that event her assets & flaws - and began to observe all of her qualities with gentleness and compassion why changing her perception.

Cleopatra was a woman who explored her intuition with a open heart and she honoured her heart and what she believed to be true.

The Queen Picks Herself Up:

A Queen never falls victim to self- doubt, because of defeat. She never stays stuck in what she can't change, because she realizes it leaves her feeling depleted.

The Queen Lives in Presence:

A Queen, a good woman lives her life effortlessly in the moment. She can sometimes be stern, but she comes back down to life and lives life in presence. Presence of tasting beautiful exquisite foods, indulging in good wines, dressing to perfection, being spontaneous, and keeping a smile upon her face.

Cleopatra was attuned to the heartbeat of the planet. She practiced using essential oils to nurture her body.

She inhaled sage to bring comfort to her soul when there was upsetting atmospheres. Cleopatra was wild and found much pleasure in living freely. Cleopatra lived on the edge & loved wildly. Cleopatra's ability to honour her femininity & bravery was undeniably potent and she received much respect in the ancient times.

The Queen Values Her Time:

A Queen a good woman makes good use of her time. She realizes life is short & as time passed we can't get back time that is lost. She invests her time in humanity and making the world a better place. Her day is full of things that bring joy & beautiful memories into her life.

She works relentlessly behind the scenes to offer society something sweet, because she believes humanity is pivotal demand and deserves valuable acts of love. Cleopatra hardly ever got involved in here say as she was too busy plotting how to make the Earth a better place.

The Queen isn't Judgement:

A Queen a good woman doesn't judge people to harshly for wrong doings, as she realizes everyone makes mistakes. She doesn't expect everyone to be opulent, to need guidance or a helping hand.

She offers her support, her kindness, with the attempt for them to see their lives headed in a better direction

The Queen Faces Her Fears:

A Queen, a good woman faces her fears & strengths even if what she's facing is less pleasing. She understands her strength is not in the situations she stays stuck in, but the situations less polished and need her urgent attention.

She understands all situations aren't prim and are sometimes hard to move away from and those situations represent her courage. She understands facing her fears makes her a stronger Queen and awakens her to endless possibilities.

The Queen Honours Her Heart:

A Queen a good woman lives in honour of the heart. She swims the subtle crashing waves of fear to understand her truth. She never does what doesn't honour her heart. She lives fully in the moment of who she is.

The Queen Is Worthy of Notice:

Cleopatra the Queen was remarkable, worthy of notice, because she was exceptional. She was the kind of Queen that had moments she felt defeated, but she was strong and she kept on fighting until there was no fight left. She didn't want the world to fear, she faced their fear for them. At times when she wasn't sure what she was doing, she believed in her heart and her heart lead to powerful intuitive secrets.

She Meditates:

Goddesses and Queens loved to spend time in nature to experience that deep drop of happiness. She understood she is Mother Earth and she contributed something beautiful to the land so her presence was vital & tantalizing.

She didn't want to be known as just appealing, she wanted to be known as abundant, and a source of love & strength.

The Queen Is Goodness:

A Queen the good woman did most gestures from the goodness of her heart, there was no ulterior motive and besides, her day was too busy to play such foolish games.

She helped other women rise above to explore greater possibilities and she felt great pleasure in opening her heart to them.

The Queen Listens:

A Queen is a good listener and practiced good listening skills to truly understand all points of view. She is logical & fair to all sides.

Back when Cleopatra ruled, a man was brought to her to be ruled upon, he had killed another to protect himself. She never held him accountable, because she thought his actions were justifiable.

He stood in front of her upset because his entourage wasn't eating, so she set him free and gave his people enough food to survive. She didn't treat him badly, because she wasn't celestial; instead, she cared for him with the compassionate heart she had.

How can you step into your Queen's energy?

A woman who is in tuned with her feminine energy radiates this abundance of energy that the world can feel and is never forgotten.

The Queen Keeps the Earth Together:

A Queen draws the earth together rather than tearing it apart. Cleopatra did everything in her power to assure that Rome & Egypt weren't in constant war. The Queen made fair decisions at her councils that benefited all sides not just the land she represented.

She was a nurturer of the land. She represented the spirit of moral order and fair judgement based on conventional rules. She had precise deception and she lived by the feathers of truth as her heart was lighter than a feather. Her thoughts filtered constant enlightenment and she was focused on reason before she would render a verdict. She is you.

You hold all these qualities.

Imagine stepping into your feminine energy as Queen and entering the deep drop that leads all the way down to the feathers of your soul. Bow your head to love, and allow all those beautiful energies to open your heart.

> ➢ Do you feel feminine?
> ➢ Do you feel vulnerable in your natural birthright?

It's okay, your birthright as a Queen is full of emotions and you are not designed to be emotionless. Do you feel secure where you are seated on the throne, my loves?

> ➢ How does it feel to be a woman?
> ➢ To just sit & allow your feelings to penetrate deep within you?

Play some soothing music.

Move your hips to the music, take a deep breath. Allow the abundance of love to transpire from your breath, take it in, enjoy it, love it, carry it with you and go out into the world, embracing your heart being light as a feather.

It is my deep pleasure to enlighten you and send you on a path that leads you home to your own authentic playground, where you dream, grow, explore, awaken, and become at one.

Wonder woman, and discover the Queen within your soul.

Memoire Of A Cortigiana Onesta

In the 16th century women were never granted permission to become doctors, lawyers, or teachers, their jobs were minimal and very low paid. Men could employ their wives and that's how most of them obtained their wealth.

Most women received their jobs through inheritance of their husband's estate.

It was divergent to see women in any profession besides food preparation, spinning cloth, housewives, domestic servants, or growing herbs and vegetables. Although, Veronica had help obtaining her status as a writer you can imagine the greatness, persistence, and talent, it took to get there.

It was hard to mistake Veronica as she displayed soft sensuality that surrounded itself in intelligence. She was poetic and intelligent; she was beautiful and fascinating. From the day she was born, she was limited in her options. A woman in her position could be a wife, a maid, a nun, or a courtesan. Veronica wanted to be a wife, but soon discovered that wasn't happening for her, so she took a detour. Let's explore her story, queens.

Veronica published a book of poems that King Henry III, was infatuated with, called **Lettere Of Importance**. This book of letters left a mark on society.

Courtesans is French came from the Italian word *"cortigiana"*, but the word was used in a variety of ways, another word for courtesan is cortigiana onesta. Veronica Franco the 16th century poet and courtesan was exactly that.

The definition of the Renaissance is the great revival of art, literature, and learning in Europe beginning in the 14th century and extending to the 17th century, marking the transformation from the medieval to the modern world.

And Veronica was the form of art used in the 16th century. Today I start with the book with her exquisite poetry that captures our heart time and time again.

I find myself locked within his eyes.

And long for, myself to know.

He hears it seems, my silent cries.

And makes my heart my reason to foe.

How can this be, to love so quickly?

"Love does not wait," is his reply.

What magic weaves his touch to trick me.

How can I now my love deny?

Veronica Franco discovered in the 16th century, skilled in literary arts, but mostly known by Venetian literati for beauty and sharp wit.

Courtesans were at the highest of the hierarchy, above madams, bourgeois, and lorettas as they represented the high-class vision of an elegant lifestyle. They were basically mistresses who lived in a realm of elegance, grace, and sophistication.

She was a true Renaissance woman who made careful distinctions when it came to her endeavours.

She was a conversationalist who loved soothing music, elegant dancing, painting beautiful art, and writing love poetry. She made a precarious living through writing. This elegant courtesan come from the Royal court where she lived.

Veronica was a courtesan who had a beautiful heart. Veronica took her own resources and financial gain to educate other women of her station. She was gifted in conversations and able to influence the town's politics with the power of noblemen in Venetian courts.

Veronica's story began when she fell in love with a man she couldn't have named Marco. Out of extreme despair she went to her mother desperately pleading, "I need this man", but she didn't befit in appearance.

Marco's father revealed to him that he sees how he looks at her, and says, "Don't underestimate loves allure Marco, enjoy it, but guard your head and your heart. You cannot marry her."

Out of obligation to the 16th century standards and his father's wishes Marco agrees.

Then meeting Veronica Marco reveals that "he must marry according to his state," Veronica asked him, "So, why are you here then?" Mario says that he just couldn't stay away.

Veronica says, "I speak of love and you speak of money."

"I speak of duty, it isn't about my heart. This is about politics; marriage isn't romance."

Veronica responded, "You have lying lips," Marco said, "If I was a liar I wouldn't tell you this."

Veronica says to Marco, "If you loved me you wouldn't say this to me period."

"But I want you," Marco responds.

Veronica said, "I'm not enough," and ran off heartbroken.

Marco asked Veronica to resign from being a courtesan, and he would take care of her. Veronica refused, because she loved him, she couldn't imagine accepting his financial contributions.

She said, "What good will that do my life; to be with you in silence?"

"If you make me your wife I will resign," but Marco still convinced the marriage would sabotage his image, declined Veronica's offer, despite being hopelessly in love with her.

Marriage in the 16th century was a business deal rather than an act of true love. Veronica never wanted to become a courtesan, but her mother told her that was the only way to receive her man's heart.

She revealed that courtesans were some of the most educated women on the planet; wrapped up in a civilized cloak.

She said, "Any chamber maid can plop down and take off her skirt, but the true power comes from something else much deeper than beauty."

Cleopatra knew that.

Aspasia, which means all others will be forgotten, but your image will remain. The spirit of beauty flows in only where the partitions are harmonious.

Her mother had been a courtesan and she truly believed Veronica couldn't obtain Marco, due to social standards unless she became a courtesan herself.

Men had to love according to their station and in the eyes of society, and Marco's father Veronica was way below the average.

She witnessed her daughter crying endlessly and she wanted to help her endure the pain, but she also didn't want her daughter to receive such a gift in wedlock.

Her mother wanted her to understand. **Theodosia**, which means supreme gift.

Also seen as an amazing woman who receives rounds of applause.

Veronica asked her mother, "How can I do such a thing?" Her mother responded, "With your mind daughter."

Her mother asked her to think of Marco, think anger, think rapture, think submission, try disdain, amusement, these are the qualities that a courtesan represents. Make him believe he is the only man in the universe.

Veronica was afraid of her vision, it was a fearless expression of her female sensuality. Full of disbelief, she says to her mother, "I'm not cut out for this." Her mother reminds her, "If you want to win you must be vulgar ostentatious, pretentious, and flamboyant.

Her mother took her to a library full of scrolls and told her, "Enfold sophistication, darling." Veronica's fascinated with the scroll selection and found herself intrigued with her new level of awareness.

 ➢ She had to become sophisticated.
 ➢ Learn how to walk gracefully.
 ➢ She had to dress elegantly.
 ➢ Learn vocabulary
 ➢ And become a woman of society.

This Venetian woman displayed a beautiful silhouette of how to come into being the most educated woman in the world.

She basically had to rise from her sleep and transform into a new beauty.

In the 16th century courtesans became a symbol of sexual liberty, beauty, and audacity.

Scandal was their middle name.

Veronica took a liking to becoming a courtesan. She began to educate the women of her station. Her mother, Paola Fracassa, educated her about the profession of honour and it was through her mother's guidance and skills in the early and late 1560s that made it possible for her to become such a lady.

Her mother had been in a relationship with Paolo Panizza, a doctor unhappy in an arranged marriage and wanted her daughter to follow in her footsteps, because she's seen the potential in living this way.

Her intellectual life came into existence when she began to share private tutorial lessons with her brother. She also became very involved in the Domenico Venier Library in Venice.

Veronica had six children only three survived past infancy. She spent most of her life living as a high-class courtesan, paying servants and raising children.

Veronica Franco mingled with cultural elite of Venice in her work of courtesan and poetry. Among other arts.

Veronica's first poetry work was published in 1550 in Venice. The first is written to King Henry III, of France and the twenty third letter was to Jacopo Tintoretto, the Venetian painter, thanking him for painting her portrait.

The letters describe the courtesan's many skills and great biographical value.

Veronica was the mistress of King Henry III and he fell in love with her through her writings. It was her one particular book that moved his heart towards her. It was her emotions, it was her vulnerability, it was her Volgograd personality, as her words were a work of art. He believed in her words so much that he gave her power that was high as his, because he truly believed she was a true Renaissance woman who could change the world. Veronica was a treasure to Venice for she lifted the nation when it felt glorious, in literature, descent in its customs.

Veronica puzzled over her feelings for an old lover.

[You went away to foreign people, and I stayed behind, the prey of the fire which, without you made my days black and sad; but as the hours progressed, little by little, I resolved a virtual and to make room in myself for others concerned. This is the true solution to my pain; in this way my mind discovered at least a cure for its deep and serious wounds; your depart for foreign lands mended the blow, although the scar could not be completely erased. Perhaps I would have been happy and not sad, if I could have enjoyed you to my heart's content, and perhaps id been happy instead. The great access of happiness might have transformed the highest joy into cruel, burdensome pain; and if gone, leaving me behind at a time full of so much delight, my distress would have had no end. So, heaven refused to my hours, joyful and serene, to avoid reducing me soon after to the worst, my most bitter pain. And I Veronica freed by heaven to such a degree, must remain content; and yet I am not able to hope that the opposite had not occurred.

On one hand, I'd prefer not to be in this beautiful place only to leave, as I did, before I properly arrived. How burdensome a good thing can become, given that the greater it is, the more grief is born in us and we must leave it all behind: the pleasure we enjoy flies quickly away; and giving no thought to pass benefit, we sadly remember only what we lost. And yet on the other hand I wouldn't want to not have seen such a beautiful dwelling. gracious and beloved to tranquility. And, although I have not enjoyed it to the full, the memory I had, the more I had cherished it, and the more I thought about leaving it would have brought me regret.

Even so, forbidding a bittersweet thought, I return in memory of the infinite delights that where there revealed to me: I have that fair side always before my eyes. And thought absent from it in my body. In my mind I still dwell them, never departing. In my heart I feel wholly reborn with such a joyful heaven on earth presents itself for her contemplation. My spirit, never quitting this place recalls its endless beauty again and again, vanquished and conquered by the highest pleasure. And why my eager spirit perceives these delights, in my own joy it brings pain to my senses...]

Veronica was forced the flee Venice due to a plague outbreak. She went back to her hometown in 1577, because she was publicly forced to defend herself against accusations of witchcraft. Although she was exonerated, she lost her assets and died in poverty. This was the moment Marco declared his love for her in front of a congregation of people to save her reputation.

I am in love with this story, Queens. I love that her mother took her aside and showed her how to be a real woman.

If you can go back to your adolescent years what would you have liked your mother to teach you?

Keep in mind, Queens, "What we love is what we resemble."

Would she tell you?

➢ Be vigorous, dear daughter.
➢ Live in the moment, dear daughter.
➢ Be courageous, and never back down, dear daughter.
➢ Be patient, dear daughter.
➢ Open yourself to new possibilities.

"Be rapturous."

That inner beauty fades and your true beauty lives in your mind?

What are you going to teach your daughter?

Here's another one of Veronica's famous poems.

["There the sea and shore sparkle, with love, who among, nereids and the sea gods, Instills sweetness Into those bring waters.

Venus encircled, by other gods still, descents from heaven to this beautiful shore, In the company of the noble graces..."]

Here is some more of Veronica's poetry to help enlighten us.

["When we too are armed and trained, we can convince men that we too have hands, feet, and a heart like yours; and although we may be delicate and soft some men who are delicate are also strong: and others, coarse and harsh are cowards. Women have not yet realized this for if they should decide to do so they would be able to fight you until death: and to prove I speak the truth, amongst so many women, I will be the first to act, setting an example for them to act."]

["I will show you my heart open in breast, once you no longer hide yours from me; And my delight will be to please you: And if you think I am to dear to Phoebus for composing poems, in the works of love. You'll find me still dearer to Venus..."]

Creator, Lover, Nurturer

We are coming to the end of our modules, beloveds', and today we begin to look at ourselves without judgement. We are going to transpire this into action by looking into our beautiful eyes and discovering our inner goddess.

Beloved, I know you are a divine goddess because you were born into the lineage of royalty. I summon you to take a closer look and merge into sovereignty.

Repeat after me. Centre yourself, love, and light a candle that entices your senses and come to understand love. You are a goddess.

I am totally capable of manifesting creativity, love, and nurturing me.

Today I believe in all my capabilities.

Say out loud three of your beautiful qualities.

I am a goddess and I have every right to feel juicy, ripe, open, vulnerable and fierce, without feeling like I've done something wrong.

Beloveds, let's start our day by balancing our inner world. Today, I send you an alkaline recipe that will nourish your body.

Coconut and Cinnamon Smoothie

> ➢ 1 banana
> ➢ 1 can of almond milk.
> ➢ 1 tsp of maple syrup
> ➢ 1/2 cup of vanilla yogurt.
> ➢ 1/4 tsp cinnamon

Today we gather to cover all derogatory limiting beliefs we told ourselves.
Repeat after me, beloveds.
My body is beautiful sexy and vital on the planet.

Today I show up to create, nurture, and love my body to give and receive pleasure.
Yes, I invite all this juiciness in.
It is ok for me to be beautiful, mysterious, and luscious.
As you dwell in the elements of the earth I hope that the day rises to greet you with love.

May the wind blow sweet nothings at your heart.

May the sun warm you up and cover you from her face.

May the moon's light brighten your day.

And may the rain fall softly against your face.

Know that the goddess will show up to love you unconditionally, because you are worth loving.

May you know that you are creator, lover, and nurturer. I hope all the pleasures of this life nurture you.

Beloveds, it is so important for us to ground ourselves from the inside out. I want this experience to be beautiful and transformative which is why I balance you through nourishing foods my love.

Recipe

> ➢ 1 cup of apples
> ➢ 3 cups of butter squash
> ➢ 1 cup of onions grated
> ➢ 4 cups of chicken stock
> ➢ Pinch of cinnamon
> ➢ Pinch of onion powder
> ➢ 1 tsp butter
> ➢ Salt
> ➢ Pepper

Today she must surrender and fight her way through, because that's all you know how to do.

Beloveds, you must surrender some more when all you want is control.

Just let it go.

Just let it go, for god knows your truth, sweetheart. You'll never be able to pick up where you left off, but the pieces will eventually come together.

Soften and accept being held when really, she feels lost and wants to be found. It's okay to want these things, just integrate them in a healthy way. Let's all do things differently.

Here is a **Dessert** to support you with your inner balance.

> ➢ 1/2 tsp of ginger
> ➢ 1 cup of pumpkin purée
> ➢ 2 cups of coconut milk
> ➢ 1/4 tsp allspice
> ➢ 1 tsp cinnamon
> ➢ 1/4 cup coconut sugar

> ➢ 1/2 tsp nutmeg
> ➢ 4 tbsp whipped cream

Beloveds, women are supposed to be emotional and feel deeply to allow the divine feminine nature to enter your heart.

We are supreme healers who are infused with creation, love, and nurturance so we can pass this inheritance into the world. You are a creator, lover and nurturer who offers love.

Live in silence, beloveds; for in silence there is not rejection and you can sit lovingly with yourself and for yourself.

Love yourself in the loneliness beloveds, for loneliness brings appreciations and fears that must be addressed.

Whoever you love, love them from a distance until you heal your pain.

Breathe your dreams into the wind, because the universe is listening.

Hold these dreams in your heart for your dreams are sacred.

Alkaline Chocolate Pudding Recipe

> ➢ 3/4 cup of coconut milk
> ➢ 3 tbsp chia seeds
> ➢ 2 tbsp cocoa powder
> ➢ 1 tsp vanilla
> ➢ 1 tsp almond butter

Beloveds, you've been listening to the same old story and it's time to understand the real story.

Repeat after me.

I'm enough.
I'm not too much.
I don't hold anyone back.

You make them bring to light the things they don't want to feel and stretch their heart in ways they would rather it not expand.

They want to be set free rather than embrace new territories.

They say being with you requires them to be something they would rather not.

Yes, we make them feel terrified, angry, untamed and insecure.

Beloveds, do you think they can take responsibility for their own actions without blaming it on us?

Because you are the creators, lovers, and nurturers, not what they said you were.

Crestor, lover, nurturer.

After a long time of feeling lack of money, how do we as a collective make money our sacred partner and supporter of our contribution to humanity?

Beloveds, many people's relationship with money is disrespectful.

Money can bring corruption, abuse, power, control, and fear.

Some of us inherit thinking that separates us from manifesting money in a healthy way.

When we inherit an unhealthy relationship with money we will often feel jealous of others who have money.

Many will avoid manifesting money in a loving way because for some their ancestors never had it, so they glue to a limiting belief that they aren't deserving.

Overwork leads to burnout

Today we tap into the creator, lover, and nurturer module.

Your voice is sacred.
Your gifts are sacred.
You are sacred.
Your ideas are worthy of notice.

You can transform your relationship with money, beloveds. You can invite wealth in, into your heart in a healthy way.

You can find inner balance, grace, and love, through this inheritance. We can change the world one human at a time through our understanding, commitment and love.

You can recreate the world.

You can call on new resources in a grounded way without fear.

You can open new dimension of thought patterns and how you draw money in.

I ask you beloveds, to make a list of all your inherited beliefs around money.

Do you believe it's a man world? Why? _____

Tell me how you feel for our discovery call.

How can you honour the divine feminine and detach from the unhealthy belief that money can't be yours? _____

Mother Earth wants the feminine to heal this perception, how can we contribute beloveds? _____

How can we step forth? _____

How can you heal the wounds? What is your contribution to mother earth's healing? _____

Rise beloveds in sovereign love and beauty, how can you bring this gift to the earth? _____

Heal your relationship with the perception of non-deserving.

Allow financial freedom to enter the sovereign queen. All queens have money beloveds, but it doesn't project fear, it doesn't arrive with strings attached. It doesn't show up with guilt, instead it shows up with love to heal the planet.

Sweet Potato Breakfast Muffin

- ➢ 1/4 baking powder
- ➢ 1 tsp baking soda
- ➢ 2 tsp cinnamon
- ➢ 1/2 cup flaxseed meal ground
- ➢ 2 cups flour
- ➢ 1 cup sugar
- ➢ 1 tsp vanilla
- ➢ 3/4 cups vegetable oil
- ➢ 3 eggs

Your Future Postcard:

Today, we begin to pause and reflect as we draw forth new energies.

Can you hear your body talking to you, beloveds?
What is she saying?
Can you feel the warning signs inside your body that something isn't right?

Tell your body; I hear you, I feel you.
I'm coming home to you, but what can I do to serve you?
Today is all about nourishing and supporting our bodies.

You have permission to love yourself beloved. and surrender to the healing power of self-love.

There is no fear in loving you. Today, we diminish fear, because it is a representation of unforgiveness, but we forgive her, so we will toss all unforgiveness to the stars.

Today is all about honouring your body and saying:

No I can't my body says I'm not into that.
I say no, because it hurts, and it doesn't feel right.
Tell negativity to go away and step into your warrior's dance.

Today mother Gaia is your healer, give her your heart.
Think of yourself walking away from what no longer serves you.

Imagine, walking barefoot rooted and grounded with Gaia and seeing your reflection in the dirt.

Creator, lover, nurturer, what do you see? _____

Carrot Soup

- ➢ 4 carrots
- ➢ 4 garlic cloves
- ➢ 1 inch of ginger
- ➢ 1/2 lemon squeezed
- ➢ 1 fresh parsley
- ➢ 1 yellow onion
- ➢ 3 cups of vegetable broth
- ➢ 1 tsp turmeric

Beloveds blend all Ingredients together to support you with your healing process.

Write down how your body shifts as you invite nutrients in.

Many people are stepping forth to claim the uncertainty in surrendering. Surrendering can often make fear arise, because in trusting in the unknown it is not clear what is ahead. It feels like giving up, but really, it's just accepting what is and what will be without expectation.

Some will discover that tears fall, because memories we wish to delete from our psyche will present themselves. In this case, we have two options, we can sit with the memories and smile inside or view it as jail sentence we want to avoid and store for later. I say store it for later, because memories never completely go away.

What often works is taking 10 seconds to face what has been drowned out, and then the next time 15 seconds, then 20 seconds, you get the drift.

If you feel a certain way it's okay, but it shouldn't be viewed as annoying or frustrating as it's just a feeling. Sometimes it's our own perceptions that keep us trapped and a little shift in our mindset sets us free to see all the things we are trapped by.

Our mind is in our mind, our hands are free, our feet are planted on solid ground and we are free to roam.

What have you been avoiding beloveds that is hard to face? _____

_____

_____

What could you face for 10 seconds?

_____

_____

What would life look like if you could remove this obstacle.

_____

_____

Goddess Kali is portrayed today with her third eye open. When she is open she allows compassion to come in, but because she represents the goddess of destruction she is often misunderstood.

Kali says It's time to wake up from our false beliefs and false ideas and take the initiative to activate our third eye.

She asks us to accept change and see the positive in it as we are going through necessary acts of destruction to make way for new beginnings.

We know deep down that the storms that have come were needed to direct change, and if it hadn't come, everything would still be the same. She had to get our attention some way, for just as soil can be revitalized, so can we. Goddess of destruction says embrace change and welcome in the chaos. Chaos is on the outside, but Kali invites us to go within.

As you accept the invitation to go within what do you discover?

_____

_____

What chaos have you been resisting to invite in, because maybe you've felt victim to the whims of what you can't understand?

_____

_____

What chaos has brought the most change and why?

_____

_____

Are you able to celebrate this chaos in anyways and if, so can you explain why for our next session?

_____

_____

Close your eyes beloved's and think of a burning question that you could use some guidance in right now.

Perhaps you are uncertain of which way to turn. What often works is going inside yourself by asking her what she needs and breathe life into her vision.

Ask the goddesses to assist you and then release by saying, "Thank you for guiding me with_____"

Write in your journal your wants and needs and trust and allow yourself to receive.

I know so many things come to mind.

Do you see yourself hugged up in love, or maybe just watching your children play at the park?

It could even be that dream job.

Whatever it is write it out.

Ask the goddesses to guide you to feel connected to who you really are and know beloveds, that your answers are divinely protected.

Your heart's longing is sacred and should be protected. It is so sacred it should be buried in the earth to be nourished as this is the beginning of your new seed that should be loved, pampered, and cared for it. Focus on the ribbon of life unwrapping your desires as you see blue skies, abundance, joy, and laughter.

The moon is calling and I'm sure you probably heard the whisper in your ear, come my dear... If you're looking for a sign this is it, you are it.

As we dive into the mystic of the moon it calls us home to pay attention to the signs from the cosmos as we claim our dreams as we lay at night. The moon is our morning rising sign to shed new light as we fade away from the old stories and breathe deeply into new visions.

Calling all daughters of the Earth, sisters of the moon to unite as mother Earth Gaia is with you. You are wild sacred and free, yet innocent and wise. The embodiment of the goddesses are elusive mysteries who knows the truth. She knows she's a healer, she knows she's a medicine woman, she knows she's the midwife, she knows she's the messenger here to nourish the Earth. The moon lends her energy, so we feel nourished and complete.

Moon Milk Recipe

- ➢ 1 cup of coconut milk
- ➢ 1 tsp of maca
- ➢ 1/4 tsp of cinnamon
- ➢ Drops of rose

Add moon milk into your bath.
Light a candle
Add; sea salt
Lemon essential oil
Pieces of sage leaves
Enter your bath

Mix all Ingredients, play some meditation music and enjoy.

Morning meditations

She wonders

Sacred earth

Her body is her precious altar.

Sitting rooted in the ground without making a sound.

Dragging her fingers along the earth she answers to the call of Mother Earth.

Nourishing her temple

Breathing deep down and connecting to her roots.

She whispers into the damp air, I love you my dear I am finally here.

Her body is her sacred temple she understands this know.
Her temple is rooted in earth.

She breathes life into her sacred Union of self- love and she crest the dirt searching for nourishment.

The words echoed like a melody, it become part of her, the words merged within her, and acts of love become her ritual.

She said," I love my body I want to be your friend and I'm sorry for the chaos and the way I dragged you through the dirt. Today, I let my innermost self unfold as she offered her devotion to the sea.

Allow your imagination freedom- it is your windows of perception so you can feel new insights, wisdom, and intuition and it will allow the windows to your soul to open. Allow new dimensions of awareness in as you meditate in the presence of the goddess.

She is listening.

She acknowledges who you are. She knows you are a child of God and the beautiful mirror of divine love. She's looked through your eyes at night while you were peacefully asleep, and she knows you are a story of chaos & love.

She knows you are most rooted when there's no clutter in the background and it becomes easier for your walls to come tumbling down. She knows you feels most beautiful when you're attuned with your heart. She knows you feels the most heartbroken when your reality is shattered; she knows you feel most heartbroken when you are spreading yourself too thin.

Relax beloveds, take a deep breath in. She knows you refuse to allow trust passers to interrupt your peace of mind.

She knows, beloveds.

I know beloved as we are in this together. She knows.

You can tell her everything; she is your divine mother who loved you from the start, beloveds.

She knows who you are, because she too been shamed out of her sensuality, because she has been made to feel dishonourable; not worthy of anything besides pain and scraps; as a result, she felt humiliated for decades. Her strength has been waning as she's felt her confidence increase and decline with age and size.

Momentarily believing the lies thinking she isn't welcomed in the world; and yet, without her the world just isn't such a beautiful loving place.

She finally knows the truth. She finally sees that beauty is the feminine way, but has been led to believe otherwise and felt so much shame about her body.

Feeling not good enough, pushed to the side. As she embraces her new metaphor she feels herself quietly transforming from the darkness into the light.

It's taken thousands of years of conditioning to break this illusion and for her to understand that those theories that were passed down aren't the goddesses' way and as she ripens all watched as those illusions fall away.

Following the guidance of her intuition is one of her strongest guides that leads to counsel and truth. When we don't listen to her guidance the call appears louder. Through resistance of her needs she becomes out of balance and her self-respect becomes wavering and she heads further away from loving herself.

Many think to become receptive the feminine must sit and receive, but receptivity is really all about deeply receiving ourselves. Receptivity is not about receiving anything from any outside source as their gifts don't make us whole and complete we do.

She is the one who trusts, trusts in her own intuition; she trusts in her guidance, she is allowing her emotions to flow through her like water flowing through a gentle stream. She is comfortable in stillness not constantly desiring to do things. She knows beloveds, that she must deeply surrender to allow acceptance and freedom to manifests in her world.

She is the one who allows breath to become her anchor that drops her out of her mind and deeper into her very own heart. She has a heart that knows so much, her heart feels so much, her heart receives so much.

As she walks, she slowly weaves the thread of the goddesses' presence into her sacred life. She has walked as the lost daughter feeling denied from the goddesses' trail. She has come to see that it was her self- esteem denying her this right as the goddesses invite her in willingly.

The goddess says, "Come my love, she who is wild and free. You are my sweet confident baby, I will stay close to your heart until you see. She who holds the power of magic and mystery in the palm of her hands. The one who's afraid to embrace the paths that scare her, afraid of the truth of her being.

"She who has walked, wounded, thirsty, and incomplete and not intimately can now be complete in me. I've been here all along my dear, but you've been afraid to face me."

How do you walk my loves? _____

Do you feel denied? _____

Why do you feel denied? _____

I need to unlock my inner wisdom, so I can receive the answers to my issues and give birth to a better version of me.

God grant me the strength I need to honour myself and my true purpose peacefully.

The courage to stand on my own.

And the wisdom to know when to let go...

My dreams are more real than my fears, and I know in you my jaded illusions disappear.

I find focus in you and It follows my dreams to become real.

Please stay with me as all my guidance comes from you.